A Melody
of
Love

Inspiration from the Beloved Hymn

A Melody of *Love*

Janice Hanna

BARBOUR

PUBLISHING

Contents

In My Heart
There Rings a Melody

I have a song that Jesus gave me,
It was sent from Heav'n above;
There never was a sweeter melody,
'Tis the melody of love.

Chorus
In my heart there rings a melody,
There rings a melody with Heaven's harmony;
In my heart there rings a melody,
There rings a melody of love.

I love the Christ who died on Calv'ry,
For He washed my sins away;
He put within my heart a melody,
And I know it's there to stay.

'Twill be my endless theme in glory,
With the angels I will sing;
'Twill be a song with glorious harmony,
When the courts of Heaven ring.

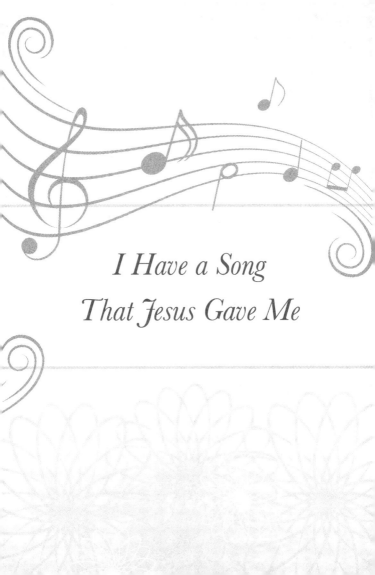

*I Have a Song
That Jesus Gave Me*

But as for me, I will always
proclaim what God has done;
I will sing praises to the God of Jacob.
PSALM 75:9 NLT

Oh, what joy! When you walk with the Lord, He places a song in your heart. It streams down from His heart to yours, a sweet melody from on high. The notes, the lyrics, the rhythm. . .they're all a part of His master plan for your life, and they were written with only you in mind.

Think about that for a moment. You don't have to go looking for this melody. You don't need to drum it up. It begins the moment you give Him your heart, in much the same way an orchestra warms up before a big performance. Perhaps the angels, in their raucous celebration above, spill over a bit of their enthusiasm. At any rate, the melody kicks in, and off you go, humming and praising your way through life, ready to face whatever comes your way. This song invigorates, brings joy, and helps keep you grounded in the Lord, even when the road gets rocky. This melody is His gift to you, after all—and what a great one it is! It stirs up hope when you feel no hope. It gives energy when you're feeling drained. Best of all, it's a constant reminder that not only is God with you, but He also resides in you, ready to equip you for whatever lies ahead. So celebrate the song, friend! Sing it with gusto and joy, enjoying every phrase, every shift in key. May His melody continue to enrich you as you grow in Him.

They will enter Zion with singing;
everlasting joy will crown their heads.
Gladness and joy will overtake them,
and sorrow and sighing will flee away.
ISAIAH 35:10 NIV

By reading the scriptures I am so
renewed that all nature seems renewed
around me and with me. The sky seems
to be a pure, a cooler blue, the trees a
deeper green. The whole world is
charged with the glory of God and
I feel fire and music under my feet.

THOMAS MERTON

*Let everything that has
breath praise the LORD.*
PSALM 150:6 NIV

Life is one grand, sweet song,
so start the music.
RONALD REAGAN

❋

Life is a song. Love is the music.
UNKNOWN

❋

Birds sing after a storm; why shouldn't
people feel as free to delight in
whatever remains to them?
ROSE F. KENNEDY

❋

Alas for those that never sing,
But die with all their music in them!
OLIVER WENDELL HOLMES

Thank You for the Song

Dear Lord, how can I ever thank
You for the song You've placed in my heart?
I sense Your presence daily, and can almost
hear the melody as it flows over me.
It gives me courage to do the very
things You've called me to do.
Praise You, Father, for giving me
a song that is uniquely mine! Amen.

God sent his Singers upon earth,
With songs of sadness and of mirth,
That they might touch the hearts of men,
And bring them back to heaven again.

<small>HENRY WADSWORTH LONGFELLOW</small>

The only thing better than
singing is more singing.

<small>ELLA FITZGERALD</small>

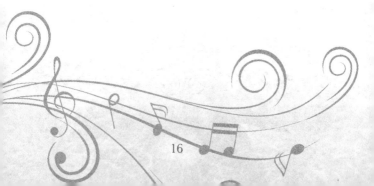

Our entire being is fashioned as
an instrument of praise. Just as a master
violin maker designs an instrument to
produce maximum aesthetic results,
so God tailor-made our bodies,
souls, and spirits to work together
in consonance to produce pleasing
expressions of praise and worship.

LAMAR BOSCHMAN

Beautiful music is the art of
the prophets that can calm the
agitations of the soul; it is one
of the most magnificent
and delightful presents
God has given us.

MARTIN LUTHER

You can cage the singer
but not the song.

HARRY BELAFONTE

I don't sing because I'm happy;
I'm happy because I sing.

WILLIAM JAMES

An Instrument of Praise

Father, when I think about the fact
that I am an instrument of praise,
personally crafted by You, it makes me
want to sing for joy! I offer myself
as an instrument in Your hands,
pliable and ready for use. Make my
mouth ready to sing praise. Amen.

God is to be praised with the voice,
and the heart should go
therewith in holy exultation.

CHARLES H. SPURGEON

Music is an outburst of the soul.

FREDERICK DELIUS

Those who wish to sing
always find a song.

UNKNOWN

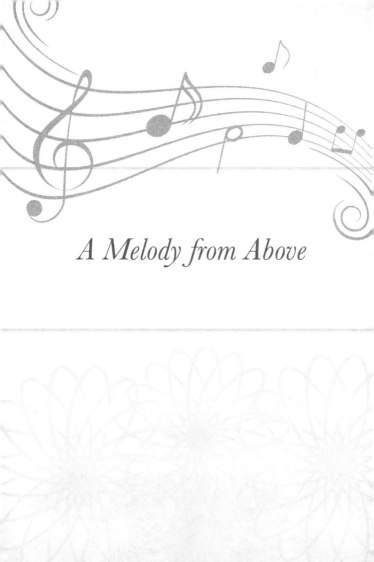

A Melody from Above

*But we are citizens of heaven, where the
Lord Jesus Christ lives. And we are eagerly
waiting for him to return as our Savior.
He will take our weak mortal bodies and
change them into glorious bodies like his own,
using the same power with which he
will bring everything under his control.*
PHILIPPIANS 3:20–21 NLT

When you think about what heaven will be like,
what comes to mind? Do you imagine streets of
gold? Glorious mansions? Pearly gates? Heaven
will have the finest of everything, after all, and the
Lord invites us to enjoy it all when we cross that

golden shore. Yes, we will see—and hear—things that can only be imagined here on earth. Did you ever pause to think about what music will be like in heaven? One can only imagine how glorious the sound when all of God's creation comes together in song. What fun, to picture all of the greatest musicians of all time, residing together, creating beautiful music together. Together, with the angels, the melodies are going to be beyond anything we can imagine here on earth. That's why it's so exciting to realize that the song Jesus has already placed in our hearts, the one He gave us the day we accepted Him as Lord and Savior, is a foretaste of that great song to come! The heavenly choir is already warming up inside of us. . .daily! Can you hear the brush of angels' wings? Do you hear the sounds of the various chords as they ring out? It is all in glorious anticipation of that great day when we will join with the saints of old to sing out our praises around the throne. Oh, join in the rehearsal! Don't put it off a moment longer. Praise Him with a heavenly song!

The experience of eternity right here
and now is the function of life. Heaven
is not the place to have the experience;
here is the place to have the experience.

JOSEPH CAMPBELL

Nothing exists without music, for the universe
itself is said to have been framed by a kind
of harmony of sounds, and the heaven itself
revolves under the tone of that harmony.

ISIDORE OF SEVILLE

Music is well said to be
the speech of angels.

THOMAS CARLYLE

Aim at heaven and you will get earth thrown
in. Aim at earth and you get neither.

C. S. Lewis

*"No eye has seen, no ear has heard,
and no mind has imagined what God
has prepared for those who love him."*

1 Corinthians 2:9 nlt

To me. . .music exists to elevate us
as far as possible above everyday life.

Gabriel Faure

Lift up your eyes and look to the heavens:
Who created all these? He who brings
out the starry host one by one and calls
forth each of them by name. Because
of his great power and mighty strength,
not one of them is missing.

ISAIAH 40:26 NIV

Heaven's Praises

Father, one of the things I'm most looking
forward to is singing Your praises in heaven
alongside loved ones who've gone before me.
What a glorious day that will be, when we
all—multiple generations of friends and loved
ones—lift our voices together in praise! Amen.

Surely it is not wrong for us to think and talk
about heaven. I like to find out all I can about
it. I expect to live there through all eternity.
If I were going to dwell in any place in this
country, if I were going to make it my home,
I would inquire about its climate, about the
neighbors I would have—about everything,
in fact, that I could learn concerning it.
If soon you were going to emigrate, that is
the way you would feel. Well, we are all going
to emigrate in a very little while.

D. L. MOODY

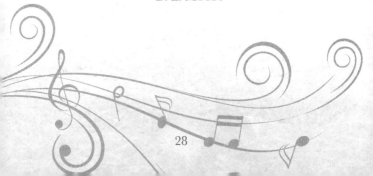

Surely that which occupies the
total time and energies of heaven
must be a fitting pattern for earth.

PAUL E. BILLHEIMER

Earth has no sorrow
that heaven cannot heal.

THOMAS MOORE

He whose head is in heaven need not
fear to put his feet into the grave.

MATTHEW HENRY

In my vision at night I looked, and there before me was one like a son of man, coming with the clouds of heaven. He approached the Ancient of Days and was led into his presence.

DANIEL 7:13 NIV

Come, let us worship and bow down. Let us kneel before the LORD our maker.

PSALM 95:6 NLT

The Greatest Worship Experience of All

Dear Lord, sometimes I try to imagine who I'll meet in heaven. Will Beethoven be there? Mozart? Musicians from my lifetime? I can almost picture all of the great instrumentalists and singers from days gone by, gathered together for the greatest worship experience of all time. What fun it will be, to add my voice to theirs!

Music is enough for a lifetime,
but a lifetime is not enough for music.

SERGEI RACHMANINOV

*

How sweet is rest after fatigue! How sweet
will heaven be when our journey is ended.

GEORGE WHITEFIELD

*

Worship changes the worshiper into
the image of the One worshiped.

JACK HAYFORD

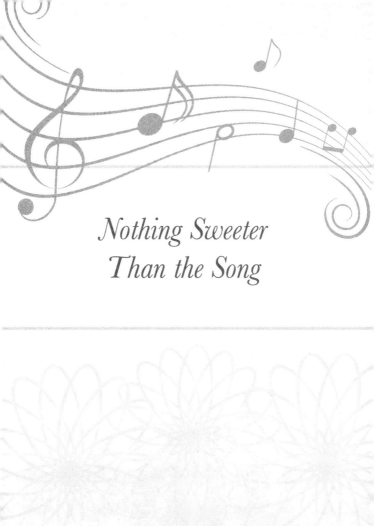

*Nothing Sweeter
Than the Song*

*When you meet together, sing psalms,
hymns, and spiritual songs, as you
praise the Lord with all your heart.*
EPHESIANS 5:19 CEV

*L*ove is like a song, if you think about it. When you love someone, there are "refrains" to your relationship. Some are sweet and easy to sing. Others are more difficult, with melodic changes. Still others float along like notes on the page, merrily dancing forward. Many are dissonant and difficult to bear. Up and down they go, pushing and pulling, tugging and loosing. To love someone, truly love them, means walking through the rough times together, clutching hands, praying, believing that the best is yet to come, even when it doesn't feel like it.

Can you sing this song—this melody of love—with those you care about? Can you keep up with the notes, even when they feel strangely out of tune or when the melody takes you in an unexpected direction? It won't always be easy to love. After all, people—even those we genuinely love—challenge us at every turn and cause us to question our ability to continue the song. But we can't give up on them, even when we feel like nudging them out of the choir! Jesus taught us by example that love, real love, lays down its life for others. It keeps on singing, even when it doesn't feel like it. It creates harmonies, even when it feels like marching to its own drumbeat. In other words, it keeps hope alive. A song like this is powerful, indeed, for it has the capacity to change lives forever.

Of all the music that reached farthest into heaven, it is the beating of a loving heart.

HENRY WARD BEECHER

"But I am giving you a new command. You must love each other, just as I have loved you. If you love each other, everyone will know that you are my disciples."

JOHN 13:34–35 CEV

There is no remedy for love but to love more.

HENRY DAVID THOREAU

Love is a friendship set to music.
JOSEPH CAMPBELL

Where words leave off, music begins.
HEINRICH HEINE

Intercessory prayer might be defined
as loving our neighbor on our knees.
CHARLES BENT

For the entire law is fulfilled in keeping this one command: "Love your neighbor as yourself."

GALATIANS 5:14 NIV

And we know that God causes everything to work together for the good of those who love God and are called according to his purpose for them.

ROMANS 8:28 NLT

Stirred to Sing

Father, I have to confess, I want to give up
on this love song at times. People can be so
difficult! They try my patience and make me
think I can't keep caring any longer. When I
feel like giving up on them, stir the notes and
cause me to sing once again. Give me Your
heart for people, Lord. Amen.

Spread love everywhere you go. Let no one
ever come to you without leaving happier.

MOTHER TERESA

To say that I am made in the image of
God is to say that love is the reason
for my existence, for God is love.

THOMAS Á KEMPIS

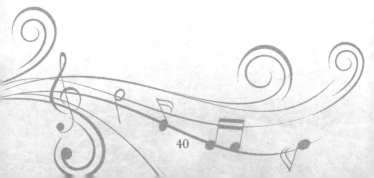

Of all the music that reached farthest into heaven, it is the beating of a loving heart.

HENRY WARD BEECHER

Bach gave us God's Word, Mozart gave us God's laughter, Beethoven gave us God's fire. God gave us music that we might pray without words.

UNKNOWN

To love means loving the unlovable.
To forgive means pardoning the
unpardonable. Faith means believing
the unbelievable. Hope means hoping
when everything seems hopeless.

GILBERT K. CHESTERTON

A loving heart is the truest wisdom.

CHARLES DICKENS

Above all, clothe yourselves with love,
which binds us all together in perfect harmony.
And let the peace that comes from Christ rule in
your hearts. For as members of one body you are
called to live in peace. And always be thankful.

COLOSSIANS 3:14–15 NLT

The Capacity to Love

Dear Lord, thank You for giving me the
capacity to love others, even when I don't feel
like it. I'm so grateful that Your Spirit resides
inside of me, giving me everything I need
when the love song of my life is difficult to
sing. I know that loving others—even when
it's hard—is Your way. Give me the words and
the music, Lord, that I might keep singing,
even when I don't feel like it. Amen.

You can give without loving,
but you can never love without giving.

ROBERT LOUIS STEVENSON

*We know what real love is because Jesus
gave up his life for us. So we also ought to give
up our lives for our brothers and sisters.*

1 JOHN 3:16 NLT

A Powerful Melody

Don't copy the behavior and customs of this world, but let God transform you into a new person by changing the way you think. Then you will learn to know God's will for you, which is good and pleasing and perfect.

ROMANS 12:2 NLT

Music is a powerful force, especially when it streams down from the Creator of all. Think about that for a moment: God, the Almighty Author of everything, created the song, the very melody, that resides within you. With just a word, He brought the oceans into existence. With a touch of a finger, mountains were created. And He's still in the business of creating. Why, even now the Lord is changing hearts, minds, and situations, with just a melodic whisper. He's transforming. Shifting. Re-creating. Don't believe it? Lean in close. Do you hear a slight shift in the melody of your life? If so, perhaps the Lord is transforming you—blowing out the dust and stirring new things. What areas of life need changing? Health? Finances? Job? Relationships? Our mighty God is capable of bringing transformation in any area that you surrender to Him. Release yourself to a shift in melody and lyrics. Surrender to a change in rhythm and pace. The Lord longs for you to be wholly submitted, ready to be changed into His likeness. What a beautiful song that will be!

Growth means change and change involves
risk, stepping from the known to the unknown.

UNKNOWN

*So all of us who have had that veil removed
can see and reflect the glory of the Lord.
And the Lord—who is the Spirit—makes
us more and more like him as we are
changed into his glorious image.*

2 CORINTHIANS 3:18 NLT

Music is a higher revelation than
all wisdom and philosophy.

LUDWIG VAN BEETHOVEN

I think worship is a
lifestyle, first of all.
MICHAEL W. SMITH

*The LORD your God will change your heart
and the hearts of all your descendants,
so that you will love him with all your
heart and soul and so you may live!*
DEUTERONOMY 30:6 NLT

Without continual growth and progress,
such words as *improvement*, *achievement*,
and *success* have no meaning.
BENJAMIN FRANKLIN

Create in me a pure heart, O God,
and renew a steadfast spirit within me.
PSALM 51:10 NIV

Give to the LORD the glory he deserves!
Bring your offering and come into his presence.
Worship the LORD in all his holy splendor.
1 CHRONICLES 16:29 NLT

The Need for Change

Dear Lord, it's so hard to admit when I need to change. I can be a little stubborn at times. But You are in the business of transforming Your people. Father, today I give you permission to change me. If the melody of my life needs to be updated, I give myself over to that process. Thank You for not giving up on me, Lord. I remain pliable in Your mighty hand. Amen.

Music washes away from the
soul the dust of everyday life.

BERTHOLD AUERBACH

When I wished to sing of love, it turned to
sorrow. And when I wished to sing of sorrow,
it was transformed for me into love.

FRANZ SCHUBERT

God grant me the serenity to accept the
things I cannot change, the courage
to change the things I can, and the
wisdom to know the difference.

REINHOLD NIEBUHR

All growth depends upon activity. There is
no development physically or intellectually
without effort, and effort means work.

CALVIN COOLIDGE

Music. . .will help dissolve your
perplexities and purify your character and
sensibilities, and in time of care and sorrow,
will keep a fountain of joy alive in you.

DIETRICH BONHOEFFER

Music can name the unnamable and
communicate the unknowable.

LEONARD BERNSTEIN

Sing praises to God, our strength.
Sing to the God of Jacob. Sing! Beat the
tambourine. Play the sweet lyre and the harp.
PSALM 81:1–2 NLT

Praise him with the sounding of the trumpet,
praise him with the harp and lyre, praise him
with timbrel and dancing, praise him with the
strings and pipe, praise him with the clash of
cymbals, praise him with resounding cymbals.
PSALM 150:3–5 NIV

Soften My Heart

So many times, Lord, I long for things in my
life to be different, for the verses of my life-
song to change. How many of those times
have I begged for change, but hardened my
heart, unwilling to be transformed into Your
image? Today, Lord, I submit to Your will.
Let change come. . .and may it begin in the
deepest recesses of my heart. Amen.

Not everything that is faced can be changed.
But nothing can be changed until it is faced.

JAMES ARTHUR BALDWIN

*This same Good News that came to you is going
out all over the world. It is bearing fruit everywhere
by changing lives, just as it changed your lives from
the day you first heard and understood the truth
about God's wonderful grace.*

COLOSSIANS 1:6 NLT

A Ringing in My Heart

*There is a time for everything, and a
season for every activity under the heavens.*

ECCLESIASTES 3:1 NIV

One of the most interesting things about the "ringing" of God's song in our hearts is that it goes back and forth, much like our heartbeat. Think of a bell, how the gong swings freely, creating a boisterous rhythm. Back and forth, louder, softer, swinging to and fro. The melody we carry within us was never meant to be monotone or dull. It's constantly on the move, swinging this way and that, as we walk through life's situations. And that's just how it should be. Nothing monotonous here! Don't some seasons of life call for a louder clanging than others, after all? Aren't some seasons quieter, filled with reverent awe? Change is a good thing when it keeps the song fresh. And we can trust the Lord with all of this. He loves us so much.

Are you going through a rough season? Listen for the change-up in the melody! Are you in an intimate season with the Lord? Surely a change in melody wooed you there. Facing a shift in relationships? Tune in to hear God's melodic instructions before you take a step. Don't resist the change. Allow it to strengthen the melody of life so that you may sing out as never before.

*My heart is confident in you, O God; my heart
is confident. No wonder I can sing your praises!
Wake up, my heart! Wake up, O lyre and harp!
I will wake the dawn with my song.*
PSALM 57:7–8 NLT

*Follow my example,
as I follow the example of Christ.*
1 CORINTHIANS 11:1 NIV

He is a wise man who does not
grieve for the things which he has not,
but rejoices for those which he has.

EPICTETUS

The seasons are what a symphony
ought to be: four perfect movements
in harmony with each other.

ARTHUR RUBINSTEIN

Freedom lies in being bold.

ROBERT FROST

Time is a dressmaker
specializing in alterations.

FAITH BALDWIN

Don't doubt the fact there's life
within you. Yesterday's ending
will tomorrow life give you.

UNKNOWN

I place no hope in my strength, nor in my
works: but all my confidence is in God my
protector, who never abandons those who
have put all their hope and thought in him.

FRANCOIS RABELAIS

The Changing Seasons

Father, I have to confess that I don't always trust You as the seasons of my life change. When I'm in winter, I long for summer. When relationships are autumn-ending, I pray for spring. Teach me to trust You, no matter the season. Keep the song in my heart alive, I pray. Amen.

*They are like trees planted along the riverbank,
bearing fruit each season. Their leaves never
wither, and they prosper in all they do.*
PSALM 1:3 NLT

*He changes times and seasons; he deposes
kings and raises up others. He gives wisdom
to the wise and knowledge to the discerning.*
DANIEL 2:21 NIV

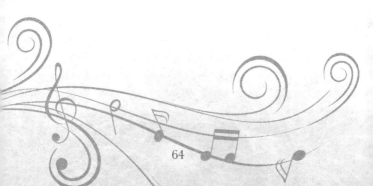

To be interested in the changing seasons
is a happier state of mind than to be
hopelessly in love with spring.

GEORGE SANTAYANA

Nature gives to every time and season some
beauties of its own; and from morning to
night, as from the cradle to the grave, it is but
a succession of changes so gentle and easy
that we can scarcely mark their progress.

CHARLES DICKENS

Music is language, just like speaking and writing are language. Its rises and falls in pitch, its fastness or slowness in tempo, its loudness or quietness in volume, and its happiness or sadness in key signature all communicate what the music is saying.

Ross W. Graham

It is better by noble boldness to run the risk of being subject to half the evils we anticipate than to remain in cowardly listlessness for fear of what might happen.

Herodotus

Shifting Seasons

Lord, I feel the rhythm of the song of my
life as the seasons shift. Back and forth
they go. Keep me consistent, Father. May
I remain bold in You as I move from glory
to glory, chorus to verse. Amen.

Expect to have hope rekindled. Expect
your prayers to be answered in wondrous
ways. The dry seasons in life do not last.
The spring rains will come again.

SARAH BAN BREATHNACH

How do geese know when to fly to the sun?
Who tells them the seasons? How do we,
humans, know when it is time to move on?
As with the migrant birds, so surely with us,
there is a voice within if only we would listen
to it, that tells us certainly when to go
forth into the unknown.

ELIZABETH KUBLER ROSS

Heaven's Harmony

Now make me completely happy! Live in harmony by showing love for each other. Be united in what you think, as if you were only one person.
<small>PHILIPPIANS 2:2 CEV</small>

It's not always easy to get along with others, even when our intentions are honorable. How awesome that the melody God placed in our hearts has the power to bring harmony! It's not divisive. On the contrary, the song inside of us is meant to draw others to the Lord and mend broken places. Need to smooth out rough waters with a friend? Tune in to the Word of God, and watch Him sing the answer over you. Looking for a harmonious ending to a rough work situation? Don't give up, even if things look impossible. The orchestra is tuning up, even now, and the music is set to begin! Listen as it smoothes out troubled places. Hope will fill the air as the message rings out. How do we play a role in this process? It's often just a matter of singing the song God's way. He always longs for us to live together in peace. Sure, we strike a few dissonant chords along the way, but passing the baton back to the Lord—the ultimate conductor—brings the whole song back into blissful harmony once again. With His help, you can manage the crescendos and the pitfalls and harmonize with even the toughest people!

*If it is possible, as far as it depends
on you, live at peace with everyone.*
ROMANS 12:18 NIV

*Blessed are the peacemakers, for they
will be called children of God.*
MATTHEW 5:9 NIV

*In peace I will lie down and sleep, for you
alone, LORD, make me dwell in safety.*
PSALM 4:8 NIV

A Harmonious Life

Dear Lord, I have to confess that living in harmony with others is tough! At work, at home, even at church, I face challenges. Thank You for giving me the courage to keep singing a harmonious song, even when those around me strike a dissonant chord! Amen.

If you want a love message to be heard,
it has got to be sent out. To keep a lamp
burning, we have to keep putting oil in it.

MOTHER TERESA

Music has charms to sooth a savage beast,
to soften rocks, or bend a knotted oak.

WILLIAM CONGREVE

Music is an agreeable harmony
for the honor of God and the
permissible delights of the soul.

JOHANN SEBASTIAN BACH

*Children, you show love for others
by truly helping them, and not
merely by talking about it.*
1 JOHN 3:18 CEV

*Praise the LORD! How good to
sing praises to our God! How
delightful and how fitting!*
PSALM 147:1 NLT

A service of worship is primarily a service to God. When we realize this and act upon it, we make it a service to men.

RALPH W. SOCKMAN

I never knew how to worship until I knew how to love.

HENRY WARD BEECHER

A Song to Unify

Father, when I get in tough situations—
and I know I will—show me what to say
and what not to say. I don't want to be a
divider. I want to be a uniter. Give me Your
heart, Your words, and Your song. Amen.

*Let the message about Christ, in all its richness,
fill your lives. Teach and counsel each other with
all the wisdom he gives. Sing psalms and hymns
and spiritual songs to God with thankful hearts.*

COLOSSIANS 3:16 NLT

*When the LORD takes pleasure
in anyone's way, he causes their
enemies to make peace with them.*

PROVERBS 16:7 NIV

Music is the great uniter.
An incredible force. Something that
people who differ on everything and
anything else can have in common.

SARAH DESSEN

Music is the melody
whose text is the world.

ARTHUR SCHOPENHAUER

Too bad people can't always be
playing music, maybe then there
wouldn't be any more wars.

MARGOT BENARY-ISBERT

Harmony is pure love,
for love is a concerto.

LOPE DE VEGA

Happiness is not a matter of
intensity but of balance and
order and rhythm and harmony.

THOMAS MERTON

Check my Heart

Lord, sometimes my motivations aren't
as pure as I'd like them to be. I say one
thing with my lips but feel another in my
heart. Help me to walk with consistency,
Father, especially as it pertains to those I
come in contact with on a daily basis.
I incline my ear toward You, Lord, as I
double-check the issues of my heart. Amen.

They say the tongues of dying men enforce
attention, like deep harmony: Where words
are scarce, they're seldom spent in vain.

WILLIAM SHAKESPEARE

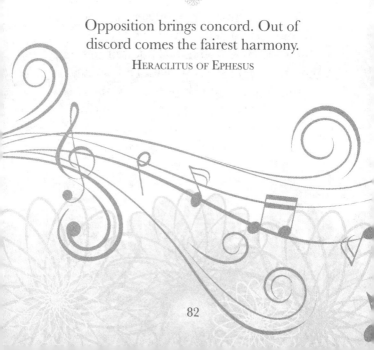

Opposition brings concord. Out of
discord comes the fairest harmony.

HERACLITUS OF EPHESUS

The Finest Soloist

*For the L*ORD *your God is living among you. He is
a mighty savior. He will take delight in you with
gladness. With his love, he will calm all your fears.
He will rejoice over you with joyful songs.*

ZEPHANIAH 3:17 NLT

$\mathcal{D}$oes God sing? If so, what does His song sound
like? Perhaps we hear it in the whisper of the wind
and the roar of the ocean. Maybe, if we listen
close enough, we pick up on the haunting refrain
as a family mourns the loss of a loved one, gone
on to be with Him. Surely we hear the celebratory

verses as He woos us into His Kingdom and as we link arms and hearts with Him.

Perhaps no other verse better conveys the idea of God singing over us than Zephaniah 3:17, where we are told that He delights in our gladness and sings over us with great joy. Wow! Close your eyes and picture that for a moment. Perhaps, at this very moment, the Almighty Author and Creator of everything, is doing a happy dance and singing a joyous song over the situation you're walking through. Oh, you're not alone, beloved! He cares enough to sing His triumphant message over you. Yes, God is the ultimate soloist, isn't He? His song carries us, in much the same way that a brisk wind carries a kite—with a light hand. Talk about a lovely wooing! A joyous wooing. A celebration of victories yet to come. We are victorious, you know. With His song leading the way, how could we ever feel defeated?

Shout for joy to the LORD, all the earth.
Worship the LORD with gladness;
come before him with joyful songs.
PSALM 100:1–2 NIV

Is anyone among you in trouble?
Let them pray. Is anyone happy?
Let them sing songs of praise.
JAMES 5:13 NIV

You Sing over Me!

Dear Lord, thank You for singing
over me! Sometimes I think I can hear
Your voice, along with the heavenly choir,
singing out the notes that give me the
courage to take my next step forward.
Thank You for a song that never ends!

There are no "if's" in God's world. And
no places that are safer than other places.
The center of His will is our only safety—
let us pray that we may always know it!

CORRIE TEN BOOM

When I think of the voice of God singing,
I hear the booming of Niagara Falls mingled
with the trickle of a mossy mountain stream.
I hear the blast of Mt. St. Helens mingled
with a kitten's purr. I hear the power of an
East Coast hurricane and the barely audible
puff of a night snow in the woods.

JOHN PIPER

God whispers to us in our pleasures,
speaks to us in our conscience,
but shouts in our pains: It is His
megaphone to rouse a deaf world.

C. S. LEWIS

In almost everything that touches our
everyday life on earth, God is pleased
when we're pleased. He wills that we be
as free as birds to soar and sing our
maker's praise without anxiety.

A. W. TOZER

Every heart sings a song, incomplete,
until another heart whispers back. Those
who wish to sing always find a song. At the
touch of a lover, everyone becomes a poet.

PLATO

There are joys which long to be ours. God sends ten thousand truths, which come about us like birds seeking inlet; but we are shut up to them, and so they bring us nothing, but sit and sing awhile upon the roof, and then fly away.

<small>HENRY WARD BEECHER</small>

But I have calmed and quieted myself,
I am like a weaned child with its mother;
like a weaned child I am content.

<small>PSALM 131:2 NIV</small>

Trusting Your Song

Lord, You are the great lover of my soul, and
I hear Your song as You sing it over me, even
now. I don't always understand the various
refrains in the song of my life, but I will walk
with You, regardless. Thank You for caring
enough about me to whisper those melodic
notes in my ear, Father. I'm so grateful
for Your direction! Amen.

I've noticed that being with you, I smile more often, I anger a little less quickly, the sun shines a little brighter, and life is so much sweeter. For being with you takes me to a different place: a place called love.

UNKNOWN

The only expenditure, and all its outworkings, for which God can be held to be responsible is that which He directs.

AMY WILSON-CARMICHAEL

It will be very interesting one day to follow the pattern of our life as it is spread out like a beautiful tapestry. As long as we live here we see only the reverse side of the weaving, and very often the pattern, with its threads running wildly, doesn't seem to make sense. Some day, however, we shall understand. In looking back over the years we can discover how a red thread goes through the pattern of our life: the Will of God.

MARIA AUGUSTA VON TRAPP

Bring the fattened calf and kill it.
Let's have a feast and celebrate.
LUKE 15:23 NIV

❋

"You alone are the LORD. You made the
skies and the heavens and all the stars.
You made the earth and the seas and everything
in them. You preserve them all, and the
angels of heaven worship you."
NEHEMIAH 9:6 NLT

Learning from Your Example

Lord, I'm so glad that You care enough
about me to celebrate over me. May I
learn from Your example and celebrate
the victories of my friends, neighbors,
and family members. May I be as happy for
them as You are for me, and may I offer up a
song of praise as readily as You do. Amen.

If we would completely rejoice the
heart of God, let us strive in all things
to conform ourselves to His divine will.
Let us not only strive to conform ourselves,
but also to unite ourselves to whatever
dispositions God makes of us. Conformity
signifies that we join our wills to the will of
God. Uniformity means more. Uniformity
means that we make one will of God's will
and our will. In this way we will only what
God wills. God's will alone is our will.

ALFONSO MARIA DE LIGUORI

Our Savior's Song

But God showed his great love for us by sending Christ to die for us while we were still sinners.
ROMANS 5:8 NLT

As you picture Christ walking the Via Dolorosa—the road to Calvary—do you envision Him singing a funeral dirge or a song of victory? The message of the cross is one of life, of salvation, of hope. In spite of the pain Jesus endured, His heart of love was evident to all who witnessed the event—both then and now. His "cross song" had one simple message: "I love you so much that I am willing to lay down My life in your place." Truly, there has never been a more poignant message. We are forever indebted to this melody, forever grateful for its lingering results. Truly, this is one song that brings not only hope for today's situations but eternal hope as well. When we ask Jesus to take first place in our hearts, the melody of the cross—the story of hope that began and ended there—becomes resident inside of it. It's as if we learn to sing in that very moment. And the song never ends. It becomes the backdrop for everything we do from that point on. The salvation message—with all of its melodic encouragement—carries us through the challenges we face. No matter what struggles we face in this life, we have the promise of the life to come. . .and all because of what Jesus did on the cross. Oh, how we praise Him for giving His life for us!

Salvation is found in no one else, for there is no other name under heaven given to mankind by which we must be saved.

ACTS 4:12 NIV

For God loved the world so much that he gave his one and only Son, so that everyone who believes in him will not perish but have eternal life.

JOHN 3:16 NLT

Calvary's Song

Father, how can I ever thank You enough for sending Your Son to die on the cross in my place? Through Him I receive not just eternal life but also a life-song that gives me hope and courage to face my daily struggles. I praise You for the cross, Lord! Amen.

For me, the backdrop of half the experiences of life includes music.

AMY GRANT

God just doesn't throw a life preserver to a drowning person. He goes to the bottom of the sea, and pulls a corpse from the bottom of the sea, takes him up on the bank, breathes into him the breath of life and makes him alive.

R. C. SPROUL

Christ is the desire of nations, the joy of angels, the delight of the Father. What solace then must that soul be filled with, that has the possession of Him to all eternity!

JOHN BUNYAN

Breezy, self-confident Christians tell us how wonderful it is to accept Christ and then have a good time all the rest of your life; the Lord won't demand anything of you. Yes, He will, my friend! The Lord will demand everything of you. And when you give it all up to Him, He may bless it and hand it back, but on the other hand He may not.

A. W. TOZER

We must have the glory sink into us before it can be reflected from us. In deep inward beholding we must have Christ in our hearts, that He may shine forth from our lives.

ALEXANDER MACLAREN

We all, like sheep, have gone astray, each of us has turned to our own way; and the LORD has laid on him the iniquity of us all.

ISAIAH 53:6 NIV

My Savior Understands

When I ponder the cross, Lord, I think
of the pain Jesus faced. My own struggles
pale in comparison, and yet I know that
He understands because of what He went
through on that wonderful, terrible day.
I am strengthened when salvation's song
grips me. I praise You, Jesus, for carrying
my sin to the cross! Amen.

Then he said to them all: "Whoever wants to be my disciple must deny themselves and take up their cross daily and follow me."

Luke 9:23 niv

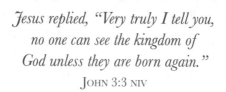

Jesus replied, "Very truly I tell you, no one can see the kingdom of God unless they are born again."

John 3:3 niv

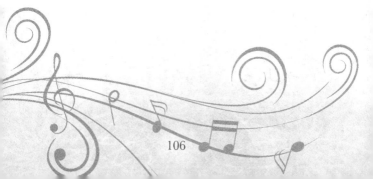

It is not thy hold on Christ that saves
thee; it is Christ. It is not thy joy in
Christ that saves thee; it is Christ. It is not
even thy faith in Christ, though that be the
instrument; it is Christ's blood and merit.

CHARLES HADDON SPURGEON

To make Jesus Lord of our life means
to surrender control of every area of
our life to Him. . . . Those whom Jesus
recognizes as His own are those who
do the will of His Father in heaven.

KEITH GREEN

*For, "Everyone who calls on the
name of the Lord will be saved."*
ROMANS 10:13 NIV

Here is a cord of love let down, and the
upper end of it is fastened to Christ's heart,
and the lower end of it hanging down the
length of your hearts. And, O! shall not
Christ's heart and yours be knit together this
day. Here is a cord to bind His heart to your
heart, and your heart to His heart.

RALPH ERSKINE

A Cleansing Melody

*Is there no balm in Gilead? Is there no
physician there? Why then is there no
healing for the wound of my people?*

JEREMIAH 8:22 NIV

A melody, played at just the right time, has the capacity to change both the atmosphere in the room and a person's mood. Research has shown that music plays a role in healing, both physically and emotionally. Don't believe it? The next time you're stressed, try turning on a soothing piece of classical music or an instrumental worship song. Ah, relief! It's almost as if you can feel the healing waters of heaven flowing over you, washing away the angst and the pain. The Lord never intended music to be anything but an expression of a grateful heart to Him. What we listen to can be a lovely reminder of the cleansing God has already done in our hearts and the healing He still longs to do. Are you in need of the healing balm of Gilead today? Do you need to wash away pain, angst, troubles? Worship Him. Let the melody of your heart—the one birthed in love from the heart of God—bring hope and healing to whatever situations life might present. When grief and despair try to raise their ugly heads, counteract them with that heaven-inspired melody. They will have no choice but to flee.

My heart, which is so full to overflowing,
has often been solaced and refreshed
by music when sick and weary.

MARTIN LUTHER

Music is the medicine
of the breaking heart.

LEIGH HUNT

There is no feeling, except the
extremes of fear and grief,
that does not find relief in music.

GEORGE ELIOT

In my deepest wound I saw
your glory, and it dazzled me.

AUGUSTINE OF HIPPO

Music is therapeutic, it can tame
a tiger and soothe a burning soul!

GEORGE NETTERVILLE

I've found that music allows years to fold like
an accordion over each other, so I guess you
don't feel the passage of time as much.

AMY GRANT

He heals the brokenhearted
and binds up their wounds.
PSALM 147:3 NIV

Sorrow has produced
more melody than mirth.
C. FITZHUGH

Take a music bath once or twice a week
for a few seasons. You will find it is to
the soul what a water bath is to the body.
OLIVER WENDELL HOLMES

A Song of Healing

Thank You, Lord, for the healing melody
You've placed inside of me. Just about the time
I think I can't bear the pain and agony that life
sends my way, Your song rises up, awakening
my heart and washing over me like a river.
Bless You for that melodic river, Father! Amen.

Shout to the LORD, all the earth;
break out in praise and sing for joy!
PSALM 98:4 NLT

What I like best about music
is when time goes away.
BOB WEIR

Life seems to go on without effort
when I am filled with music.
GEORGE ELIOT

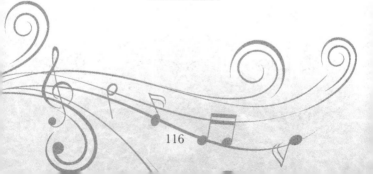

Singing becomes
a form of therapy.

PLACIDO DOMINGO

Where words fail, music speaks.

HANS CHRISTIAN ANDERSEN

Such songs have power to quiet
The restless pulse of care,
And come like the benediction
That follows after prayer.

HENRY WADSWORTH LONGFELLOW

When I hear music, I fear no danger.
I am invulnerable. I see no foe.

HENRY DAVID THOREAU

Each time he said, "My grace is all you need.
My power works best in weakness." So now
I am glad to boast about my weaknesses, so
that the power of Christ can work through me.

2 CORINTHIANS 12:9 NLT

Comforted by the Song

Father, I'm so grateful for Your counsel
during the difficult seasons. You lift my
spirits and give me Your eyes to see my
situation as You do. How can I ever
thank You for the comfort You bring?
Praise You for keeping the song alive,
even when I don't feel like singing. Amen.

Music is the art which is
most nigh to tears and memory.

<small>Oscar Wilde</small>

And the God of all grace, who called you to
his eternal glory in Christ, after you have
suffered a little while, will himself restore
you and make you strong, firm and steadfast.

<small>1 Peter 5:10 niv</small>

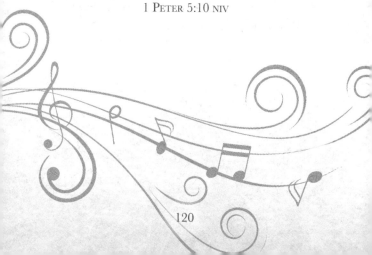

Music is the moonlight in
the gloomy night of life.

FRIEDRICH RICHTER

*He refreshes my soul. He guides me along
the right paths for his name's sake.*

PSALM 23:3 NIV

But for you who revere my name,
the sun of righteousness will rise
with healing in its rays. And you will
go out and frolic like well-fed calves.

MALACHI 4:2 NIV

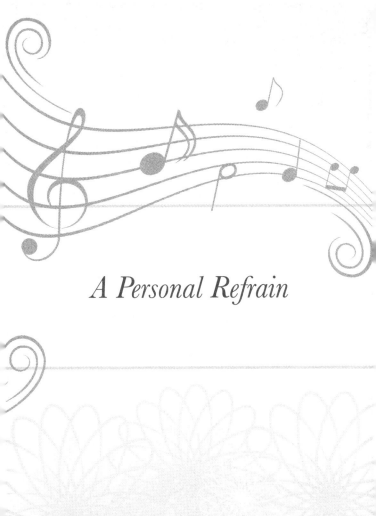

A Personal Refrain

Here I am! I stand at the door and knock. If anyone hears my voice and opens the door, I will come in and eat with that person, and they with me.
REVELATION 3:20 NIV

A song with my name in the title? One dedicated just to me? Is such a thing possible? It is, when you consider the fact that the song God places in each of our hearts is a personal, private one. Listen closely. Can you hear it? He's whispering the melody into your ear, even now. Stay tuned in. Listen closely. Those lyrics, that melody, the strange and unusual arrangement of notes on the page. . .He uses them to woo you to Himself, and to direct you to where you need to go. As Revelation 3:20 says, God stands at the door of our hearts and knocks. He's a perfect gentleman. He won't crash the door down or force you to sing His song. Instead, He gently nudges and woos, hoping we will respond. And when we do—when we catch sight of the fact that He has singled us out—what joy follows! For a personal, one-on-one relationship with the Lord is truly beyond anything else we've experienced in this life. Where else can we find someone so interested in our needs, our hopes, our dreams? God stands today at the door, a song on His lips, a melody in His heart, ready to stir us to action. Will you answer? Will you join in the song?

While others still slept, He went away to pray
and to renew His strength in communion with
His Father. He had need of this, otherwise He
would not have been ready for the new day.
The holy work of delivering souls demands
constant renewal through fellowship with God.

ANDREW MURRAY

There is delight in singing,
though none hear beside the singer.

WALTER SAVAGE LANDOR

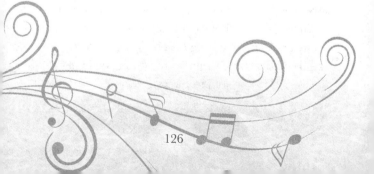

The soul which has come into intimate contact with God in the silence of the prayer chamber is never out of conscious touch with the Father; the heart is always going out to Him in loving communion, and the moment the mind is released from the task upon which it is engaged, it returns as naturally to God as the bird does to its nest.

E. M. Bounds

Music is nothing separate from me. It is me. . . . You'd have to remove the music surgically.

Ray Charles

None do seek the Lord so earnestly, but they have need of stirring up to seek him more earnestly; neither have any attained to such a measure of communion with God, but they have need to seek for a further measure.

Hear this, you kings! Listen, you rulers!
I, even I, will sing to the LORD; I will
praise the LORD, the God of Israel, in song.

JUDGES 5:3 NIV

Listening for the Song

Lord, so often I hear You knocking at my
heart's door, but I'm so busy! Life interrupts
our time together. Today, I slow down to listen,
Father. I won't make You wait any longer!
I run into Your arms and listen to the song
You sing over me. Thank You for desiring
one-on-one time with me, Lord! Amen.

Every soul is a melody
which needs renewing.

STEPHANE MALLARME

*We proclaim to you what we have seen and
heard, so that you also may have fellowship
with us. And our fellowship is with the
Father and with his Son, Jesus Christ.*

1 JOHN 1:3 NIV

Some days there won't be a
song in your heart. Sing anyway.

Emory Austin

Flower

If you cannot teach me to fly,
teach me to sing.

Unknown

Verse sweetens toil, however rude the sound;
She feels no biting pang the while she sings,
Nor as she turns the giddy wheel around,
Revolves the sad vicissitudes of things.

WILLIAM GIFFORD

I can't remember a
time when I wasn't singing.

DINAH SHORE

An Energizing Refrain

Father, when I'm drawn into Your presence, when I slip away from the chaos of my day-to-day life, I'm energized from within! For those moments—those hours—there is no pain. There are no haunting memories. There is only sweet fellowship and communion with the One who sees all and knows all. Praise You for sweeping me away with the song You've written just for me! Amen.

The branch of the vine does not worry, and toil, and rush here to seek for sunshine, and there to find rain. No; it rests in union and communion with the vine; and at the right time, and in the right way, is the right fruit found on it. Let us so abide in the Lord Jesus.

HUDSON TAYLOR

You have been used to take notice of the sayings of dying men. This is mine: that a life spent in the service of God, and communion with Him, is the most comfortable and pleasant life that anyone can live in this world.

MATTHEW HENRY

Everlasting Song

*And I saw what looked like a sea of glass
glowing with fire and, standing beside the
sea, those who had been victorious over the
beast and its image and over the number of its
name. They held harps given them by God and
sang the song of God's servant Moses and of the
Lamb: "Great and marvelous are your deeds,
Lord God Almighty. Just and true are your ways,
King of the nations. Who will not fear you, Lord,
and bring glory to your name? For you alone are
holy. All nations will come and worship before you,
for your righteous acts have been revealed."*

REVELATION 15:2–4 NIV

Sometimes we get tired of certain songs and move on to others. Perhaps we hear the lyrics or melody so much that it gets old. Isn't it miraculous to realize that the song Jesus placed in our hearts will never grow old? We won't want to "change our tune," as it were. No way! Instead of finding it wearisome, the melody will become dearer as the days go by. As we reach our golden years, the desire to sing grows stronger still. And can you imagine crossing over glory's shore, singing all the way? What an amazing thought—we have been given an everlasting song! "Holy, Holy, Holy is the Lord God Almighty, who was, and is, and is to come!" (Revelation 4:8 NIV) It's not just for the here and now; it's for all of eternity. In some respects, we're only singing the first few verses here. The melody—crystal clear and beautifully sweet—will invigorate us as we gather around the throne of God, ushering up praises that can only be imagined in this life. Doesn't that give you chills? Oh, sing! Make melody in your heart, for that melody will one day usher you directly into His throne room!

I can safely say, on the authority of all that is revealed in the Word of God, that any man or woman on this earth who is bored and turned off by worship is not ready for heaven.

A. W. TOZER

This grand show is eternal. It is always sunrise somewhere; the dew is never all dried at once; a shower is forever falling; vapor is ever rising. Eternal sunrise, eternal sunset, eternal dawn and glowing, on sea and continues and islands, each in its turn, as the round earth rolls.

JOHN MUIR

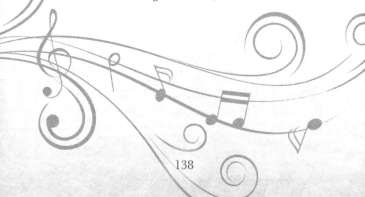

*For in the day of trouble he will keep me
safe in his dwelling; he will hide me in the
shelter of his sacred tent and set me high upon
a rock. Then my head will be exalted above
the enemies who surround me; at his sacred tent
I will sacrifice with shouts of joy; I will sing
and make music to the L*ord.

PSALM 27:5–6 NIV

All the way to heaven is heaven,
because Jesus said, "I am the way."

ST. CATHERINE OF SIENA

Death is the golden key that
opens the palace of eternity.
JOHN MILTON

I have come home at last! This is my
real country! I belong here. This is the
land I have been looking for all my life,
though I never knew it till now. . . .
Come further up, come further in!
C. S. LEWIS

A Heavenly Song

Dear Lord, thank You that death is not a thing to be feared, but a transition from one life to another. Your heavenly song woos us to a place where there is no more pain, no more sorrow. Praise You, Father, for such a place! Amen.

This is a place where grandmothers hold babies on their laps under the stars and whisper in their ears that the lights in the sky are holes in the floor of heaven.

RICK BRAGG

I thank my God for graciously granting me the opportunity of learning that death is the key which unlocks the door to our true happiness.

WOLFGANG AMADEUS MOZART

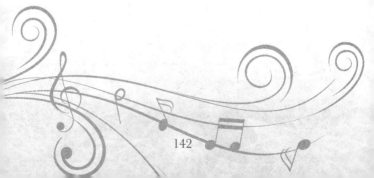

He who binds to himself a joy
Does the winged life destroy;
But he who kisses the joy as it flies
Lives in eternity's sun rise.

WILLIAM BLAKE

For death is no more than a turning
of us over from time to eternity.

WILLIAM PENN

If a single glimpse of him on
earth affords you profound delight;
it must be, indeed, a very sea of bliss,
and an abyss of paradise, without a
bottom or a shore, to see him as he is;
to be lost in his splendours, as the stars
are lost in the sunlight, and to hold
fellowship with him, as did John the
beloved, when he leaned his head upon
his bosom. And this shall be thy lot, to see
the Lamb in the midst of the throne.

CHARLES SPURGEON

An Everlasting Melody

Father, thank You for placing an everlasting song in my heart. It doesn't just invigorate me now, in this life. It stirs me up and makes me excited about the next. When I think about singing praises in heaven, my heart is stirred as never before! I can't wait for that day, Lord. Amen.

Christian, here is joy for thee; thou hast looked, and thou hast seen the Lamb. Through thy tearful eyes thou hast seen the Lamb taking away thy sins. Rejoice, then! In a little while, when thine eyes shall have been wiped from tears, thou wilt see the same Lamb exalted on his throne. It is the joy of the heart to hold daily fellowship and communion with Jesus; thou shalt have the same joy in heaven; "there shalt thou see him as he is, and thou shalt be like him."

CHARLES SPURGEON

"Holy, holy, holy is the Lord, the all-powerful God, who was and is and is coming!"
REVELATION 4:8 CEV

A Foreign Song

*But how can we sing the songs of
the L*ORD *while in a pagan land?*

PSALM 137:4 NLT

We live in a fallen world. People around us don't always understand our passion for God or appreciate the song He has placed in our hearts. Still, we must go on singing, even when others ridicule or raise an ugly fist. In a sense, we are foreigners. Aliens. In 1 Peter 2:11 (NIV) we are given insight into this: "Dear friends, I urge you, as foreigners and exiles, to abstain from sinful desires, which wage war against your soul." Temptation to do the wrong thing—to sing a different song—will hit us at every turn. But we must remain strong in the Lord and continue to be a representation of Him to those who are lost. How do we do that? By staying close to Him. By worshiping and reading the Word. By keeping the song that He's placed in our hearts alive. Yes, we are odd, by the world's standards. But one day every knee will bow, and every tongue confess that He is God. Until then. . . keep singing, beloved. Keep singing.

Through Jesus, therefore, let us continually offer to God a sacrifice of praise—the fruit of lips that openly profess his name.
HEBREWS 13:15 NIV

Music acts like a magic key, to which the most tightly closed heart opens.
MARIA VON TRAPP

You've gotta dance like there's nobody
watching, Love like you'll never be hurt,
Sing like there's nobody listening,
And live like it's heaven on earth.

WILLIAM W. PURKEY

Act as if what you do makes
a difference. It does.

WILLIAM JAMES

But how can they call on him to save them unless they believe in him? And how can they believe in him if they have never heard about him? And how can they hear about him unless someone tells them?
ROMANS 10:14 NLT

In the same way, let your light shine before others, that they may see your good deeds and glorify your Father in heaven.
MATTHEW 5:16 NIV

Reaching Others with the Song

Lord, I'm pretty sure some of my friends don't "get" me. They don't understand my relationship with You or the worship songs that rise out of me. I know You've placed me where I am—near the people I'm supposed to reach with Your love. Stir up a new song inside of me, one filled with longing to reach out to those who don't know You. Give me the courage to sing, even when others are not. Amen.

Be as a bird perched on a frail branch that she feels bending beneath her, still she sings away all the same, knowing she has wings.

VICTOR HUGO

But when you get music and words together, that can be a very powerful thing.

BRYAN FERRY

I am a little pencil in the hand of a writing God who is sending a love letter to the world.

MOTHER TERESA

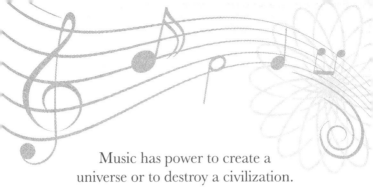

Music has power to create a
universe or to destroy a civilization.

KATHERINE NEVILLE

*So is my word that goes out from my mouth: It will
not return to me empty, but will accomplish what I
desire and achieve the purpose for which I sent it.*

ISAIAH 55:11 NIV

A melody is not merely
something you can hum.

AARON COPLAND

For I am not ashamed of the gospel,
because it is the power of God that
brings salvation to everyone who believes:
first to the Jew, then to the Gentile.

ROMANS 1:16 NIV

This is the true joy in life—being used
for a purpose recognized by yourself as
a mighty one; being thoroughly worn out
before you are thrown on the scrap heap;
being a force of nature instead of a feverish
selfish little clod of ailments and grievances
complaining that the world will not devote
itself to making you happy.

GEORGE BERNARD SHAW

Letting My Light Shine

Lord, I don't want to hide my light under a
bush because I'm afraid of what others might
think. I don't want to hum my life-song in
the quiet recesses of my closet. Give me the
courage to openly express what You've given
me to share with others, I pray. Amen.

On my account you will be
brought before governors and kings
as witnesses to them and to the Gentiles.
MATTHEW 10:18 NIV

God's way is perfect. All the LORD's
promises prove true. He is a shield for
all who look to him for protection.
PSALM 18:30 NLT

Corporate Praise

For he said to God, "I will proclaim your name to my brothers and sisters. I will praise you among your assembled people."
<small>HEBREWS 2:12 NLT</small>

Lifting up songs of worship during our private prayer time is so powerful, isn't it? But this isn't the only time we let the melody ring out. There's so much power in corporate worship. Standing alongside brothers and sisters in the Lord. Rejoicing in blissful harmony. All hearts, eyes, and thoughts focused—not on one another, not on life's problems, not on conflict or pain—on Him. It's true, what we read in Deuteronomy 32:30, that one can put a thousand to flight, but two, ten thousand. "There's power in numbers," as the old saying goes. We need to learn to take advantage of this principle when we're in a corporate worship setting. The next time you're gathered with fellow believers, lifting up the Lord in song, keep this in mind. Instead of analyzing the songs or fretting over the style of music, listen. Truly listen to the wonderful sound of dozens—perhaps hundreds—of fellow believers, all united. Focused. Worshiping. Ah, what joy!

A bird does not sing because it has an answer. It sings because it has a song.

CHINESE PROVERB

I trust your love, and I feel like celebrating because you rescued me. You have been good to me, LORD, and I will sing about you.

PSALM 13:5–6 CEV

What then shall we say, brothers and sisters? When you come together, each of you has a hymn, or a word of instruction, a revelation, a tongue or an interpretation. Everything must be done so that the church may be built up.

1 CORINTHIANS 14:26 NIV

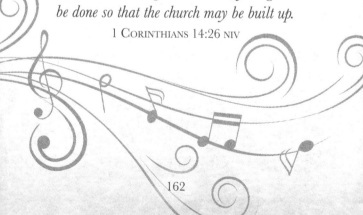

When God's people begin to praise and worship Him using the Biblical methods He gives, the Power of His presence comes among His people in an even greater measure.

GRAHAM TRUSCOTT

Let the message about Christ, in all its richness, fill your lives. Teach and counsel each other with all the wisdom he gives. Sing psalms and hymns and spiritual songs to God with thankful hearts.

COLOSSIANS 3:16 NLT

If we are going to worship in Spirit, we must develop a spirit of worship.

MICHAEL CATT

*God is Spirit, and those who worship
God must be led by the Spirit to
worship him according to the truth.*
JOHN 4:24 CEV

*It is imperative that the Christian, at the
beginning of his pursuit to understand what
true worship is, gets it clear that the object
of our worship is to be God and God alone.*
R. C. SPROUL

Worshipping as One

Lord, thank You for the opportunity
to worship side by side with fellow
believers. What joyous songs we sing!
I'm so grateful for those harmonious
moments, when all disagreements are
laid aside and we focus solely on You.
Come and dwell among us, Lord! Amen.

A friend knows the song in my heart
and sings it to me when my memory fails.

DONNA ROBERTS

It is in the process of being worshipped that
God communicates His presence to men.

C. S. LEWIS

Music is the universal
language of mankind.

H. B. LONGFELLOW

*I praise you, LORD, for answering my prayers.
You are my strong shield, and I trust you
completely. You have helped me, and I will
celebrate and thank you in song.*
PSALM 28:6–7 CEV

The time has come for a revival of public
worship as the finest of the fine arts. . . .
While there is a call for strong preaching there
is even a greater need for uplifting worship.
ANDREW W. BLACKWOOD

Our Lord and our God,
we praise you and kneel down to
worship you, the God of holiness!
Psalm 99:5 cev

The Lord says, "Then I will heal you of
your faithlessness; my love will know no
bounds, for my anger will be gone forever."
Hosea 14:4 nlt

The God of All Harmony

Father, You are the God of all
harmony! Thank You for showing me
how to sing alongside others, even those
I don't always agree with. Whether we're
united in song or facing challenges, You are
there in our midst. I'm so grateful for the
melody of love You whisper in my ear as
I add my praise to theirs. Amen.

Until I arrive, be sure to keep on reading the Scriptures in worship, and don't stop preaching and teaching. Use the gift you were given when the prophets spoke and the group of church leaders blessed you by placing their hands on you. Remember these things and think about them, so everyone can see how well you are doing. Be careful about the way you live and about what you teach. Keep on doing this, and you will save not only yourself, but the people who hear you.

1 Timothy 4:13–16 cev

A Powerful Song

In everything we have won more than a victory because of Christ who loves us. I am sure that nothing can separate us from God's love—not life or death, not angels or spirits, not the present or the future, and not powers above or powers below. Nothing in all creation can separate us from God's love for us in Christ Jesus our Lord!
ROMANS 8:37–39 CEV

The Lord encourages us through song. He lifts our spirits and convinces us that we are more than conquerors, no matter what we're facing. Going through a tough time? Lift your voice in worship. Facing a health crisis? Sing out a new song to the Lord. Through the words of the song He places in the heart of His people, God conveys truth: We are more than conquerors through Him who loves us. There's truly nothing this life can present—sickness, pain, angst, job problems, financial woes—that can separate us from His love. But we need to be reminded of that, which is why keeping a song on our lips is so powerful. Sing on, friends! Don't let the storms wash you away. Praise your way through them. And as you sing, envision yourself triumphant, victorious. You are, you know. In Him, you are more than a "survivor." You are a thriver!

Music is the voice that tells us that the
human race is greater than it knows.

NAPOLEON BONAPARTE

*But you are not like that, for you are a chosen
people. You are royal priests, a holy nation,
God's very own possession. As a result, you can
show others the goodness of God, for he called you
out of the darkness into his wonderful light.*

1 PETER 2:9 NLT

Our God, you are the one who rides on the clouds, and we praise you. Your name is the LORD, and we celebrate as we worship you.

PSALM 68:4 CEV

Music gives a soul to the universe, wings to the mind, flight to the imagination and life to everything.

PLATO

*Christ gives me the
strength to face anything.*
PHILIPPIANS 4:13 CEV

*For the Spirit God gave us does
not make us timid, but gives us
power, love and self-discipline.*
2 TIMOTHY 1:7 NIV

A Song That Invigorates

Heavenly Father, I feel the power of Your song inside of me, invigorating and giving courage to do things I never thought I could do before. Thank You for strengthening me from the inside out. With praise comes courage! With praise comes joy and confidence. With praise I understand that, with You, all things are possible! Amen.

You gain strength, courage, and confidence
by every experience in which you really stop
to look fear in the face. You must do the
thing which you think you cannot do.

ELEANOR ROOSEVELT

Although the world is full of suffering,
it is also full of the overcoming of it.

HELEN KELLER

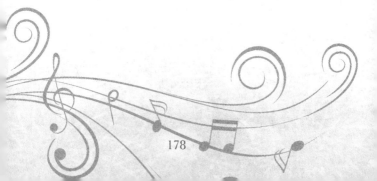

The greater the obstacle,
the more glory in overcoming it.

MOLIERE

*Children, you belong to God, and you have defeated
these enemies. God's Spirit is in you and is more
powerful than the one that is in the world.*

1 JOHN 4:4 CEV

The LORD is my light and my salvation—
whom shall I fear? The LORD is the stronghold
of my life—of whom shall I be afraid?
PSALM 27:1 NIV

If you are distressed by anything external,
the pain is not due to the thing itself, but to
your estimate of it; and this you have the
power to revoke at any moment.

MARCUS AURELIUS

The Overcoming Song

Thank You, Lord, for the reminder that in You, I am powerful. I don't have to sit idly by. I will speak words of faith and begin to triumph, even when it seems impossible. Oh, I praise You for the overcoming song that resides within me! Amen.

Sooner or later, man has always had
to decide whether he worships his
own power or the power of God.

ARNOLD J. TOYNBEE

*Don't be afraid. I am with you.
Don't tremble with fear. I am your God.
I will make you strong, as I protect you
with my arm and give you victories.*

ISAIAH 41:10 CEV

My One and Only

Because your love is better than life,
my lips will glorify you.
PSALM 63:3 NIV

If you've ever been in love, then you understand the phrase, "That's our song." Couples often have a particular love song that drew—or kept—them together. Beloved, God is your one and only, your one true love. At any given point in your journey with Him, the two of you will have songs that mean the world to you because they are melodies that have strengthened your relationship.

Think back over your journey with the Lord. Can you think of three or four songs that stand out— songs that drew you to His presence, consoled you, or lifted your spirits during a troubling time? Perhaps you've tried playing those songs for friends or loved ones, only to have them shrug and say, "Sure, that's a fine song." They don't get it, do they? It doesn't touch them in the same way. That's all right! They don't have to get it. Our job is to recognize and respond to the songs that the Lord sings over us. Those melodies call us back into His courts when we're busy. They draw us, even when we think we don't have enough hours in our day. They cause time to stand still, even when everything around us is spinning out of control. Today, thank the Lord for those special "one and only" songs that the two of you have shared. They are your Savior's personal gift to You, His bride.

We love because he first loved us.
1 John 4:19 niv

*God loves each of us as if
there were only one of us.*
St. Augustine

A Wooing Song

Dear Lord, I sense Your love as never before.
It stirs my heart and woos me to Your inner
courts. That love gives me joy and strength
and reminds me that You care about me as
an individual. Thank You for loving me in
spite of my flaws, Father! Amen.

Because God has made us for Himself,
our hearts are restless until they rest in Him.

AUGUSTINE OF HIPPO

Music expresses that which cannot be put into
words and that which cannot remain silent.

VICTOR HUGO

But the man who is not afraid to admit
everything that he sees to be wrong with
himself, and yet recognizes that he may be
the object of God's love precisely because of
his shortcomings, can begin to be sincere.
His sincerity is based on confidence, not in
his own illusions about himself, but in the
endless, unfailing mercy of God.

THOMAS MERTON

The love of God is greater far than tongue or pen can ever tell. It goes beyond the highest star and reaches to the lowest hell.

FREDERICK M. LEHMAN

Though we are incomplete, God loves us completely. Though we are imperfect, He loves us perfectly. Though we may feel lost and without compass, God's love encompasses us completely. . . . He loves every one of us, even those who are flawed, rejected, awkward, sorrowful, or broken.

DIETER F. UCHTDORF

After silence, that which comes nearest to
expressing the inexpressible is music.

ALDOUS HUXLEY

The greatest honor we can give
Almighty God is to live gladly because
of the knowledge of his love.

JULIAN OF NORWICH

O love of God, how rich and pure!
How measureless and strong!
It shall forevermore endure the
saints' and angels' song.

FREDERICK M. LEHMAN

Your Great Love

Father, I never understood love until I accepted Your version of it. I'd tasted so much of what the world called love, but it never truly satisfied. Now that I've spent time in Your courts, nestled next to Your heart, humming the song You placed inside of me, I see what I was missing all along. Praise God, it is missing no more! I'm so honored You have called me Your own. I will forever sing Your praise! Amen.

The LORD is my strength, the reason
for my song, because he has saved me.
I praise and honor the LORD—he is my
God and the God of my ancestors.

EXODUS 15:2 CEV

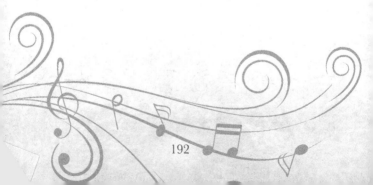